MW01492923

Look Up!

See Heaven in the Clouds

Look Up!

See Heaven in the Clouds

Mary Soliel

Boulder, Colorado

Look Up!
See Heaven in the Clouds

Copyright © 2015 by Mary Soliel

Twelve Twelve Publishing, LLC, books may be ordered through booksellers or Amazon.com.

Twelve Twelve Publishing, LLC

P.O. Box 822

Louisville, CO 80027 U.S.A.

www.twelvetwelvepublishing.com

alighthouse@mac.com

Logo Design: Lisa Kubik

Because of the dynamic nature of the Internet, any Web addresses or links contained in this book may have changed since publication and may no longer be valid.

ISBN: 978-0-9890169-1-9

TO SCOTT AND KAREN

Who fully accept
their mother's constant need to look up,
always believing in her work,
while gently reminding her to
watch
where she is walking.

CONTENTS

ACKNOWLEDGMENTS

I thank all of the fabulous people who have supported my work, especially through social media. You know who you are. You found my cloud picture taking and sharing contagious, and many of you were looking up like never before, too. You were a very important part of the driving inspiration behind this book. I extend special gratitude to the wonderful photographers who generously provided permission to use their extraordinary captures among my collection of photos.

In addition to my beautiful kids and my lovely friends who have personally supported me, as previously acknowledged in my prior books, my profound appreciation goes to Archangel Michael and my angel support team. They showed me the way every day, and continue to teach me so much. They told me to "Look now!" or "Leave now!" and, thus, guide me to astounding and miraculous discoveries. And now, through this book, and as one of the many pioneers of our evolving world, I intend to get as many people as I can to *Look Up!* and experience the magic and miracles for themselves.

INTRODUCTION

Our world is changing much faster and more profoundly than we can possibly be aware of. We simply cannot see all that is going on behind the scenes as we create our new earth, our Heaven on earth. However, we can look upward if we wish to open our hearts for a preview. Look out your window right now. Most would believe it's just the same ol' sky you see every day. But it isn't by a long shot. The skies are speaking to us. They are revealing what we call Heaven. Clouds are being "painted" with faces, beings, colors, and symbolism of all kinds, which mirror the promise of, and journey toward, our new and Heavenly earth.

The veil between Heaven and earth continues to thin, and revealed are all kinds of ethereal gifts. This book will help you to literally see with your own eyes what the Heavenly realms are showing us. You will learn to understand and feel their messages through the clouds. When we look up, we grow our understanding of our metaphysical existence and the evolution of our very beings. We also feel our way toward this new age. We merely need to look up and feel the comfort, peace, and awareness that only Heaven can provide.

When we keep an open mind to the possibilities before us, we grow our desire to step into the magnificence of who we really are—our souls. The skies are leading us to our ultimate reunion with ourselves as we truly learn to see clearly now. You may already have this awareness of the skies, and this book serves as a validator to what you know. Either way, I'm thrilled for your presence here.

There is a rapidly growing awareness that our skies have changed due to less than positive influences, as well—specifically from chemtrails (different from contrails). People are noticing their skies unusually streaked with white lines sprayed from jets. This subject will be briefly addressed in Chapter Four. While we still reside on a planet of both Light and dark energies, the Light is winning. And as we raise our vibrations as a people and a planet, all atrocities will eventually cease.

Part of our spiritual awakening is acknowledging the truth of what is occurring on earth and in our skies, including the darkness. We cannot keep our heads in the sand. We must learn about and protect ourselves from the poisons in our air, food (especially gmos), water, etc., as best as we can, while seeing it all from a higher perspective, and remaining in a state of love and not fear. The world is full of extreme dichotomies, and this is certainly true regarding our skies and what we see when we look up. *But Heaven is upstaging the darkness while reminding us that we are supremely watched over.*

I invite you to view this book from this perspective. We still exist in a world of duality, and we must see the whole picture, even these polarizing opposites, in order to truly understand what is happening on our planet, as well as within each of us as we evolve with it. This book's goal is to focus on the positive and help you embrace great excitement and faith that we are indeed moving further into love and Light. It will prove that we have plenty of help from "above" who join us in this unprecedented journey.

Until we shift fully into our new Heaven on earth, both Light and dark energies will coexist on earth, and in the sky, to varying degrees. Therefore, please consider this book to be a study, an observation of a new phenomenon. It absolutely does not claim to have all the answers; this subject is complex. I have documented not only what I have observed on my own, but also, and more significantly, messages and formations that were shown to me for the purpose of sharing with you. These pictures are ultimately a celebration of the pioneering path to our Divine destiny, for those who choose to consciously walk it.

My greatest challenge in creating this book was choosing among the thousands of pictures I've taken to document and celebrate the magic of what we see when we look up. On any given day, I could easily take fifty or even upwards of a hundred pictures. There were days that were simply extra magical and I was grabbing for my camera with unbridled exuberance. The second greatest challenge was knowing when to stop adding to this book. I hope to create a sequel to *Look Up!* as I have no doubt that the magic quotient will be on the rise and there will be astounding new discoveries to share with you.

As you will notice, in many cases I did not spoil the surprise of what I see in each of the pictures throughout this book. For the most part, you will first see the picture, and then following the image I reveal the specifics of what I see and wish to share with you. But you may see something completely different. We all do see so differently, so it is important to have the chance to discover on your own. This book is designed to be read in order. Please take your time viewing each photo first, before reading the paragraph(s) below it. With that said, here we go. Thank you from my heart for taking this magical journey with me, into the wondrous, beckoning unknown.

CHAPTER ONE:
I CAN SEE CLOUDS CLEARLY NOW

My desire to look up was especially inspired by seeing this beautiful display on one sunny afternoon in New Mexico, in July of 2009.

My kids and I traveled to our beloved home away from home, and spotted this heart-shaped cloud in the sky with much excitement. The three of us knew, immediately and without question, that the formation of this particular cloud was not some form of coincidence. It carried much meaning, and we knew that we were supposed to see it. And feel it! Oh, how we adored what we felt was a gift from the angels.

We moved to gorgeous New Mexico—dubbed most perfectly as "The Land of Enchantment"—the summer before the dawn of the new millennium, and that rich experience grew our love for all that we see when we look up. New Mexico's big skies with striking cloud formations commands one's relentless attention, as well as the sun's enchanting light gracing the land like nowhere else I've ever seen. Colorado is so beautiful too, where we eventually moved to five years later, and we continue to enjoy the skies from the Rocky Mountain vantage point. [Note: I was in a coffee shop editing this very chapter. When I left, the first license plate I spotted in the parking lot was a New Mexico plate with the word "SKY" on it. Synchronicity is a most marvelous validator and mirror.]

Looking back more than a decade, I recall I had this strong desire to photograph New Mexico's skies, the clouds in particular, and make picture cards out of the images. I never did follow that prodding. But to me it was telling, because I feel I knew on some level that I would do work in this area. But the skies simply weren't "ready" back then. The veil had not thinned enough to display the magic, until more recent years.

It was the cloud shapes that I noticed first in my journey to understand the changing and increasingly magical skies. After this first sighting, I began to see more clouds shaped as hearts. Sometimes they were inverted, where the blue sky defines a heart shape from the boundaries of the clouds. I also saw angel-shaped clouds quite regularly and knew, intuitively, that they presented messages to those whose eyes happened upon them.

In February of 2011, I saw yet another heart-shaped cloud, but for the first time this cloud revealed something extremely intriguing. I literally saw faces in the cloud! It was undeniable. In particular, I saw an old man's face with a definitive moustache and beard. I immediately knew that I was embarking on an exciting new discovery—and yet I was very calm about it, as if I had been prepared somehow for what I witnessed. (The heart cloud on page 1 has faces too; however, I didn't notice them back then.) It was later that year when my understanding of the changes in our skies reached a tipping point.

On the morning of November 24, 2011, my journey towards these new insights really began in earnest. I stepped outside my back door and was amazed to see a cloud with what seemed to have a distinct hole cut out of it. I had never seen anything like it. I recently learned that this unique appearance is technically termed as a "fallstreak hole."

It wasn't until I saw the following close-up that I realized—and I mean *immediately* realized—how incredibly special this cloud was. Not everyone sees who I see, but many have. When I share with audiences in my presentations, about half of the attendees can see the very famous person in the image on the next page. Please note that this is the only photograph in the book that I tampered with in any way outside of cropping. The photo is presented in sepia, versus in full color, which will help you to see his face.

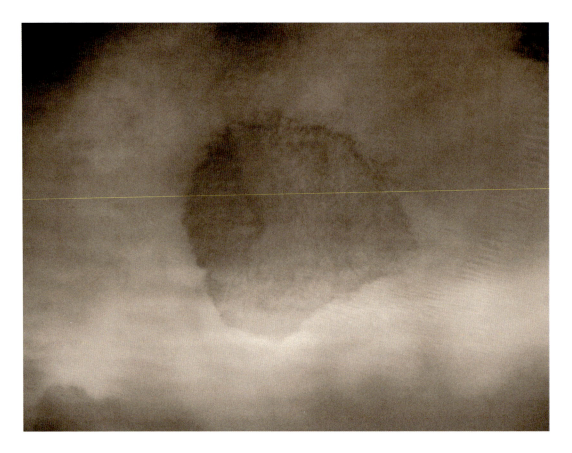

Yes… it's Albert Einstein! Do you see him? Can you see the hair outline, his right eye, nose, and moustache? What is he doing in the sky? Did the great and powerful soul of Einstein literally reveal his face in the clouds? I believe that souls, like that of Einstein, as well as our angels, Archangels, Ascended Masters, and guides, are helping us perhaps far beyond our understanding and awareness during these evolutionary times. It is all part of a most grand design to help guide us through this shift of the ages.

Do I believe that the soul of one of the world's greatest minds purposely made this appearance, knowing that I would be sharing this picture with others? Absolutely! Beings in Heaven know exactly who is watching and when. *And they are seeking messengers to spread the word of their presence among us, one of whom may be you.*

It is no coincidence, of course, that I just now took a break in writing, went online to a social networking site, and the top post in the feed is by someone who posted: "Coincidence (said Albert Einstein) is God's way of remaining anonymous." Splendid synchronicity—or *meaningful* coincidences—validates just what we seek to understand.

Specifically, this synchronicity validated yet again my experience with the Einstein cloud. I say "yet again," because around the time that I saw this cloud, I also saw signs of Einstein everywhere else. His profound quotes and pictures of him were synchronistically appearing before my eyes. My book *I Can See Clearly Now: How Synchronicity Illuminates Our Lives*[1] describes the phenomenon of synchronicity through twelve years' worth of my personal synchronistic experiences. Spreading the awareness of this constant miraculous force of the Universe is one of my greatest passions, and it certainly plays a perpetual role in what we see when we look up.

Let me share another example of why I'm convinced that beings know without a doubt just who is looking up. The sighting displayed on the next page hit home on a very personal level.

I was hiking on a hilly path in Boulder, Colorado, and, luckily, I had my picture-taking iPhone with me. The sky was especially beautiful since the sun was about to set, but because I was looking towards the sun, I was unable to see what the sky was uncovering. I "heard" that I should snap several pictures though, and, as always, I listened. [Note: When I use the word "heard" in quotation marks throughout this book, I am referring to a telepathic hearing, from my unseen Heavenly friends.]

Immediately afterwards, I reviewed the photos on my phone and was utterly stunned to realize what I had captured. I saw my own face! Just below the small green orb (within the light magenta eye-shaped orb which also shows up often in solar captures with the iPhone) is the inside corner of my left eyebrow and eye. Then my hair, both eyes and eyebrows, and the beginning of my nose come into view. I know this sounds so grandiose, but I truly saw myself in this cloud, and still do every time I view this picture.

This photo is brimming with many other faces. Do you see them? Take your time and soften your gaze as they come into view.

---

[1] Soliel, Mary. *I Can See Clearly Now: How Synchronicity Illuminates Our Lives.* Lincoln: iUniverse, 2008.

Directly above the green orb is an image of a man, superimposed with what I believe to be my image. You can see his left eye, nose, forehead, and hair. Our images blend together. This blending/superimposing of faces is often seen when looking up. And superimposed yet again is a large face of another man, very handsome, and he takes up more than the whole upper left quadrant of the image. Clearly revealed are his huge, stunning eyes, nose, and mouth. His face is larger than the other faces described thus far.

As if this weren't compelling enough, there is yet another gem revealed in this same image. Look directly at the sun. You will see on each side a pair of lips about to kiss, and the lovers' lips form somewhat of a heart shape at the top of the sun. There are also many other faces to be seen all around this image. I've returned to this photo so many times, often seeing a new face I hadn't noticed before.

Needless to say, I quickly deemed this photo as my favorite capture. That is, until I saw the following life-changing cloud, which became the cover photo of this book.

I looked out my kitchen window on June 24, 2013 and saw this most uniquely shaped cloud. I simply knew that it was incredibly special. So I went to get my camera and ran outside as fast as I could, before it changed—something I do quite often. What I saw first was this long nose and I immediately thought of the Shroud of Turin, a treasured image I have hanging in my home. I then heard the words, telepathically: "Yes, it is Me."

Do you see the image of Jesus in this cloud? Look first for the nose in the upper center, and tilted. The rounded top part of this cloud is His whole, crowned head, which leans to our left. What made this sighting especially powerful and undeniable was that I was personally aware of a very powerful healing and ceremony taking place halfway around the world to help release the Christ Consciousness to this planet—just hours from the time this photo was captured. I was in awe, humbled, and it was a moment I will never forget.

There is nothing like the firsthand experience of seeing something with your very own eyes and feeling it in your own heart, when it is placed right into your personal life experience. This book strives to open your eyes to these possibilities, as they are for everyone to witness. Once aware and accepting of this phenomenon, you will enjoy—or, hopefully, have already enjoyed—your own miraculous sightings.

It may appear irrational to consider that a cloud's message can be so personal. But you can say the same thing about synchronicity. When a meaningful coincidence touches you on a deep and intimate level, the astronomical odds involved may initially lead you to question that it's truly for you, perhaps struggling to accept the grandiosity of it. The key is to get out of your head and into the wisdom of your heart, which tells you that it is real. And you merely need to surrender to the magic and gifts of the Universe.

This is why it is so important to share with others. When we share our mystical experiences, it seems to activate the possibilities for everyone involved, and the heightened awareness causes endless ripple effects.

These were a few of those clouds that truly changed my life, because the profundity of the messages was undeniable. As time went on, my cloud sightings revealed more and more magic. But before we get to that, let us explore how to see the magic.

CHAPTER TWO:
HOW TO FIND FACES IN THE CLOUDS

How do we embrace the magic in the skies? First, we have to release fears of the unknown by surrendering to any apprehension over the mysterious, and just be excited about the adventure that awaits us each day that we beautifully choose to look up. Your choice to purchase this book tells me that you are indeed curious and excited. So here we go.

On any given day, you may discover a face or even scores of faces in the clouds above. They usually look very realistic; some appear comical, like caricatures. Let us begin with exploring the faces. Because once you see the faces, they will cause you to see the skies in a whole different way. Once you accept that the skies are alive with communication from Heaven's beings to us human beings, there is no going back. And that is a good thing. Because you are a pioneer discovering a new world up there, which is mirroring the new world we are creating down here, on earth.

Here are some things to keep in mind when looking up, especially when seeking faces in the clouds, and most easily seen via a photograph. You may choose to return to the sunset photo on page 6 to practice some of the following steps:

Look up with an open heart and mind.

When you look up, imagine that you are on another planet looking up into its atmosphere and seeing it for the first time. Because in effect, that is what you are doing as the skies are no longer the same. Our eyes are conditioned to see what we expect to see, so we need to open up to the new.

Look for the eyes first.

Scan the photo. You may see a pair of eyes, or literally dozens of pairs of eyes, even in a single cloud. It is easiest to begin with finding the eyes. Focus on just one pair for now. Simply look for two circles or ovals close together that represent a pair of eyes of a certain shape and size. Once you see the eyes, the whole face comes into view. You may even see a full or partial representation of a body. But more often it's just the faces—from lifelike to even comical looking ones.

Look for the superimposed, holographic representations of beings.

Once you see a face, another one may come into view, and then more and more, one on top of another… truly superimposed. Soften your gaze at the photo and allow the visions to reveal themselves. Don't rush it, as it may be an unfolding. You can squint your eyes as an artist would, as that may help to pinpoint the focus on any one area.

Take a break and return to the photo for a second look.

When you take a second look at your photo, chances are you will see it at least somewhat differently, or even in a totally fresh new way. That one face that was so obvious in the original gander is one you now cannot even locate! This is the magical quality of the holographic and artistic beauty of these cloud presentations. Also, you may even see more than you did with the first look.

Any camera will deliver.

The vast majority of photos seen in this book were taken with my easily accessible iPhone. While my son gifted me with a DSLR last year, which I treasure, most of my sky photos were taken with my iPhone, simply because of the time factor (i.e. no time to focus or use settings). I always desire to capture a photo instantly, before the clouds change, as they often rapidly do. An expensive camera while great for quality is not necessary, as any kind should work just fine.

Express gratitude.

Whenever you see a splendid sight, feel gratitude in your heart. Gratitude brings forth more to be grateful for. Get excited about it and you will attract more miracles into your life. This goes for all desirable aspects of your life experience, of course.

Embrace your inner child.

Allow yourself to see and respond with the curiosity and exuberance of the child that is still within you. Be in a state of joy and playful surrender as you ponder the skies. Just as children learn through play, we can choose to not take life as seriously and embrace the gifts of surrender.

Listen to the nudges.

Some of my best captures occur when I follow the whispers from my angels to "Leave now." I know to take my camera, go outside, and there is always some amazing sight. This happens quite often, and I'm never disappointed and rather filled with gratitude for the Divine guidance. Since my main camera for cloud sightings is my phone, I usually have it with me. Sometimes I hear the whisper to "Take a picture now" even though I cannot see anything significant in the moment. And I find myself later amazed by the gift of mere listening. Oftentimes I stop my car en route to snap a picture since I'm always seeing treasures up there while (carefully) driving.

We *all* have the ability to hear messages telepathically, but we aren't taught this. I believe that our angels are whispering to all of us. We suddenly know to turn left and not right, to sit here and not there (for a destined meeting, perhaps), or to buy this product and not that one. This truly is not a gift for the few, but rather everyone. Consider the possibility that you may not have met your soul mate, chose the work you do, or ended up in the town you did had you not listened to those whispers of guidance. Our angels cannot interfere with our free will without our permission. We must simply ask for help, and they can help us in profound ways. Once we are conscious of the help we receive, we can use it regularly and to our great and blessed advantage. Those in the Heavenly realms see the whole picture. They see so many things that we cannot.

Listen for a message.

In those moments when you feel a cloud is meaningful to you, consider that there is a personal message and just listen. Imagine connecting not from your mind, but from your heart. You may hear a message with your actual ears, or receive it in a telepathic manner. It may be a single word or many words. I created a YouTube video that explains in a simple manner how you can channel your angels (search the "MarySoliel" channel on YouTube.com). It is becoming increasingly easier to channel, and it is everyone's Divine birthright to do so, including yours, whether you would choose to practice it for your own benefit and/or to help others.

Share your findings with others.

When you share your photos with another, you may wish to let them first find the faces or consider the symbolism themselves. Often you will help each other to see things you had not previously noticed.

Expect to enjoy an improved day.

By looking up and acknowledging the magic in the sky, it actually raises our energetic vibration. We simply feel good as our moods, thoughts, and expectations improve. When this happens we attract positive experiences, thoughts, and feelings, and this raises our vibrations so easily and effortlessly. Frankly, I believe that even greater things are occurring, such as activations with certain sightings and higher communications that our souls understand. We are all on this grand learning curve together which is unfolding step by step.

Take pictures of clouds, even if you don't see anything noteworthy.

You may see something special when looking directly at the cloud, or you may not. You may even see something looking through the camera's viewfinder. Or, perhaps you will not see anything noteworthy until you download your picture onto your computer (for best viewing)—and the latter happens quite often to me. *Sometimes the faces can only be seen digitally via a photograph, and not with the naked eye.* So please keep that in mind if you desire to take random photos of clouds.

In this particular case, I immediately and unexpectedly saw a man's stunning profile (towards the center of the lower right quadrant of picture) while hiking, and snapped several shots. You can see his profile defined by his eye, strong nose, thin moustache (look for a thin dark line angled toward the somewhat leafless branches), and mouth. It wasn't until I downloaded the photo that I saw the other faces to the left of him.

Sometimes the juxtaposition of beauty among the ordinary creates the extraordinary.

While I usually attempt to make my photos "picture perfect" by not having telephone wires or homes or the artificial competing with the view, sometimes their inclusion can help create a more extraordinary picture as we see the expected along with the unexpected, if you will.

CHAPTER THREE:
LETTERS, NUMBERS & SYMBOLS, OH MY

The following sighting proved reason enough to include this chapter.

On January 13, 2014, I simply went out to get the mail and was astounded to see the most beautiful word in our vocabulary written in the sky, right above my home. Do you, too, see the word "love" in the clouds on the prior page? I've seen letters, numbers, symbols, and more so many times, but never before had I seen the whole word "love."

I adore spotting clouds that are shaped as words, or even as a letter here or there. I might feel driven to decode a message by working with my intuition, and often the message is immediate. Even if there is only one stand-alone letter, there may be a meaning attached. Letters, numbers, and symbols in clouds can have a completely different message for one than they do for another. The same goes for when an identical synchronicity occurs for many, and yet separate and specific messages may be deemed by each receiver.

For example, people all around the world are repeatedly catching 4:44 and 11:11 (and other number combinations) on the clock. I discuss this phenomenon in my books, as well as in articles. My article on the 444s on hubpages.com has over 200,000 hits. That alone tells me that a lot of people are experiencing the same and seeking answers. But, the personal meaning for catching these numbers on the clock—or on a sign, address, receipt, etc.—can express something specific to each individual, based on timing and their life situations. So that is something to consider. I believe it's our angels who are getting our attention by nudging us awake or whispering to us to look at the clock "Now!" perhaps without our realizing that it is them. The experience is magical.

The day of September 14, 2014 surely proved magical, and it was also an important one for this chapter. I woke up in the wee hours and went to work on the manuscript of this book. As I contemplated the "love" cloud that introduces this section, I literally asked the angels for more numbers and letters in the sky to capture for this very chapter. Then I went back to sleep.

I had a vivid dream where I drove somewhere to meet with my Canadian friend and healing artist, Lisa Kubik. Lisa also has a great interest in the skies. I consider her to be my "cloud confidante." In the dream, as soon as I got out of my car to greet her, a man nearby excitedly asked us to look up. There were clouds clearly shaped as numbers. I woke up quite amazed since I dreamed up what I had asked the angels for—more number clouds.

Before I go further, let me first explain that I am a channel of Archangel Michael, meaning I literally receive messages from him for the purpose of writing channeled books about the Heavenly earth that we are creating. The communication between us is via telepathy.

After waking, and even though I was busy doing something, I "heard" from Archangel Michael to tell Lisa "right now" about the dream. So I messaged her immediately. At the time, Lisa was visiting northern Alberta. She had read my message while outside. And just as she was about to reply to me with a message via her phone, she looked up at the sky and took a picture.

Photo by Lisa Kubik

After capturing this stunning image, she realized that her name "Lisa" was written in the sky! Not only was this a most profound moment for her and what appeared to reveal to her a cosmic message about her gorgeous artwork, but also it happened right after notifying her of my dream as well as my request of the angels. I received the letter-shaped clouds picture that I asked for through my dear friend in a most magical way that awed us both. How synchronistic is that? Granted, Lisa was about 1500 miles from where I am and yet distance, of course, didn't matter. A synchronistic miracle was occurring at the same time as some kind of universal setup. This experience further opened my mind to ways that *our angels are painting the skies with very personal messages.* They are asking us to just look up, and this can bring forth astounding miracles for all those willing to see.

It was exciting to see a letter in combination with a beautiful sun image.

I entitled this photo "Angels are Love," as the sun seemed to help form a most beautiful angel cloud next to the letter "L." Another seeker may have seen this in a whole different way. It's always interesting to share and find out what another sees in the same visual.

When I was talking to my son, Scott, about some dreams I have for the future, a response to this discussion was revealed only minutes later in a most unexpected way. I went to my kitchen window to look up and had to do a double take, and then rushed to get my camera.

Do you, too, see the word "slow" in the very center? (There are lots of faces everywhere, as well.) Was this a synchronistic message I needed to heed, that I must slow down and not rush into anything? If that weren't enough, the very next time I looked out the window (about 20 minutes later), I saw a truck displaying the huge word "SWIFT" driving in *reverse!* Okay, Universe… I got it.

I asked my angels, yet again, for more representations of numbers and letters in the sky. The very next day I looked up and saw a very obvious 5 near the sun, along with a smaller 1. When you see numbers in the sky (or anywhere, for that matter), they could be referring to a date or time possibly, and they always carry a numerological meaning. Every number carries a specific energy, and the science of numerology assigns meaning to each number. I include a chapter about numbers in my book *I Can See Clearly Now*. It explains that the number 5 is known to stand for good surprise change. And the number 1 signals new beginnings. Sometimes the meanings are personal, as well.

Then on my birthday in October of 2014, I "heard" to look up and saw this display of numbers. Surprisingly, I could clearly see the numbers 1, 2, and 3 just below the sun, even though it was very bright.

When you repeatedly come across numbers in ascending order, whether they are seen in the sky or on a receipt or a car's license plate right in front of you, for example, it's a positive sign. You are moving in the right (ascending) direction. Whereas if you experience the opposite and the numbers are in descending order, it could (but not always) be mirroring a different message which may prompt you to reassess your thoughts or choices. The world is indeed our mirror and this mirror shows itself in endless ways in the sky, as well as on earth.

Over the years, I've seen scores of clouds shaped as exclamation points, and they often underscore what is going on in my life. Either something exciting is happening simultaneously and they validate my thoughts at the moment I see them, or they are a preview that something wonderful and, perhaps, profound is about to occur. This first one has an angelic feel, to me.

Something to keep in mind is that there may be a theme of messages in the sky and/or on the earth supporting each other at the exact same time, or within a close period of time. They may together be validating a particular message, thus it behooves you to "connect the dots." Often signs are repeated again and again through different messengers, and that gives the receiver more confidence in their assessment.

Here, an exclamation point is highlighted right next to a heart-shaped cloud. So it was very easy to connect the dots in this case. This was a most exciting sight to behold, and it had a significant impact on how the rest of my day unfolded. These are the joys that stem from simply looking up.

CHAPTER FOUR:
SEEK THE MESSAGES OF CLOUDS

You may have spotted a cloud in the shape of an angel, which is especially thrilling. Or perhaps a feather, a person, or even a magic lamp. Maybe you've noticed a cloud shaped as a word, a number, or an exclamation point. What is the message being delivered to you? Is it a message from your guardian angel? Is it that you are about to take flight in your life? Is it drawing attention to someone or something in your life that you need to take notice of? Go with your intuition regarding the meaning behind the portrayal. Don't miss the opportunity for a potential message for you. But if you do miss it, or if you don't understand the message, you can simply ask your angels and the Universe for another sign. And expect that sign to appear, but without attachment or expectations of how or when the sign will be revealed.

One of the most profound validations of my work and mission in this life was represented by a spotting of two clouds formed like perfect angel wings on each side of the sun, as I described in *I Can See Clearly Now*. These types of intensely meaningful, once in a lifetime sightings, feel as if God is speaking right to you. Again, they are for each and every one of us to enjoy, not a so-called "special few." Yet, we must be aware and remain open to the messages so that we do not miss out on these Divine gifts.

There are many aspects to this awareness. A most significant one is that of timing and in conjunction with what some may refer to as *meaningful* coincidences (there is no such thing as mere coincidence). However, I prefer Carl Jung's term, "synchronicity." Synchronicity is often directly involved with a cloud sighting. This miraculous phenomenon illuminates, guides, validates, and blesses your life on a daily basis, but it requires your awareness of this usually silent messenger. And the timing of a cloud sighting is often essential to the message, so always consider it.

For instance, if you are calling out to God for help, and minutes later you look up in the sky and see a cloud shaped as an angel, you may choose to acknowledge the synchronistic gift which demonstrates that you are indeed heard and watched over. Many of us know that we are never alone, as our angels are always with us, but sometimes that visual reminder is a very welcomed gift. That same cloud symbol can be meaningful in a different way to another observer, perhaps for someone who never believed in angels.

It will become second nature to consider the timing of your own thoughts when you spot a certain gem up there, because you'll find again and again that there is often a stunning connection. If you are consumed by thoughts about possibly accepting a new job opportunity or pursuing a new life in a different geographical location, and you keep seeing bird-shaped clouds, for example, maybe it's a message to set flight for a new beginning.

There will be times when you feel that a cloud is just for you. In fact, the gift can be an absolute life changer when you feel it on such a deep and personal level. I hope you have experienced, or will soon experience, your own miracle in a cloud.

Of course, not every cloud proves meaningful. I use my intuition to discern and decipher what does and does not have meaning to me. And timing is one of those aspects that come into play.

The following story is a great example of how key timing is in cloud spotting, and in regards to deciphering synchronistic messages, as seen in *I Can See Clearly Now*.

"Do you think that those in the Heavenly realms can give you clear and direct messages by writing them in the sky? Clouds are one of my favorite signs. I believe they speak volumes— such as the time I flew to Denver and then took a van from the airport with nearly a dozen people on the way to Breckenridge to attend a spiritual conference. We all were stunned to see a magnificent stream of clouds that together perfectly formed an image of an angel with arms spread wide open as if welcoming us. When we arrived at our destination, we saw that the theme of the conference had to do with angels, and the promotional signs, badges, and programs all featured an image of a beautiful angel."

Synchronicity is an unstoppable energetic force delivered by the Universe, and oftentimes by your angels. It comes through an endless variety of messengers including people, places, animals, signs, numbers, the time on the clock, license plates, nature… and magical clouds.

As I alluded to earlier, it is both fun and rewarding to also consider the surprise effect of capturing cloud pictures for no particular reason. Sometimes, I merely take a picture and wait until I return home and look at the downloaded image on my computer screen to find out what I actually captured. Or, other times I get clear nudges to take pictures, even when I don't see anything special.

This is exactly what happened when I captured this photo. I observed the fast moving clouds but didn't see the surprise awaiting my notice, until later. Do you see what I see in the bottom right quadrant?

In this case, I was quite surprised by a very clear and remarkable image of an alien (look first for the large eyes, then bulbous head, neck, etc.). This excited some of my friends and acquaintances while others were taken aback, even a little disturbed by it. There is more to be seen in this photo, but the alien is most striking.

Let's look at some ways that clouds are used to deliver messages to us:

The arm wavers.

As funny as this may sound, beings are often seen waving at us! It appears to be a way to get our attention when we see some direct offshoot in the form of a limb, conspicuously coming from a cloud. I've seen this occur so many times, and often at the most meaningful times. It sure gives the skies a most friendly feel.

On Mother's Day of 2013, my kids took me for a drive which gave me the perfect opportunity to capture this gem when crossing through the heart of Boulder. I couldn't help but utter "To infinity and beyond!"

A few months later, my kids and I decided to get away and spend some time boating on a lake, and as soon as we pulled out of the driveway, we saw this guy in the sky.

It felt as if he was saying, "Bye… Have a great time!" It sure brightened up our day for some fun and relaxation.

One spring morning, I felt to walk out of my garage which I was cleaning, and look up, and was amazed by what was right in front of me. I went back to work feeling more joy and positivity, to say the least.

In this case, it looks like an angel wing waving at the setting sun.

And, in fact, when I saw this stunning cumulation of clouds, it seemed to display angelic royalty. You are looking at the profile of her face (hair, eye, nose, mouth, cheek, and ear), as if standing to her side, and complete with crown. You may see it differently since we all see and perceive in our own individual ways.

I often see beings that seem to be dancing, clearly intending to express movement. And this is how I imagine the Heavenly realms, with beings generally moving and very alive, even more alive than humans on earth. This is why I never understood or use the phrase "rest in peace." I believe that once we transition to Heaven, our souls do anything but rest, for the most part. Our souls are set free of the physical bodies that can hinder movement for many reasons, and in many ways.

Angels.

This treasure was taken in December of 2011, when visiting Naples, Florida.

Do you see the profile of a kneeling angel with head bowed and hands seemingly clasped in prayer? Her wings extend from the left of her head, outward. She knelt before many of us traveling on a busy road in Naples. I couldn't help but wonder how many looked up and noticed the marvel. It's with great joy that I could capture this beauty and share with you here.

I saw this angel while driving near my home. When I first saw her, it looked as if she was playing a harp, but by the time I was able to stop and photograph her, the harp disappeared and her arms were raised. This was a being expressing herself in a fluid way.

Here is my absolute favorite cloud picture of an angel. I was snapping several pictures of the sun on May 22, 2013. At the time, I was in a parking lot walking toward a store when I heard Archangel Michael ask me to take a few more pictures. Since I was looking straight at the sun, I couldn't see much of anything, until I looked at my phone. And then I was promptly stunned!

I knew it was Archangel Michael himself, recognized as the "Angel of the Sun," making his presence known to all future viewers of this picture. You can see his face just to the left of the sun, and his body, including an angel wing to our right, off his shoulder.

Right after I saw Archangel Michael in a cloud, I saw this little cherub.

When you experience an angel sighting, it may cause you to feel it in your heart as much as you see it with your eyes. I hope you already know just what I mean.

Even when I come across a cloud that may not be perfectly shaped, I go by the feelings I have when spotting one such as this. I could strongly sense an angelic presence, which seemed to be offering something to the observer.

The following display would probably be referred to as a "sylph." Sylphs are considered to be mythological spirits or elemental beings of the air. Whatever you name them, I hope you find this to be beautiful and comforting.

The eyes have it.

Do you see something especially striking in this photo? And once again, I didn't see "it" until I loaded the photo onto my laptop, and it was a wonderful surprise.

When you look really closely, you may spot several beings in this image, particularly on the right side of the photo and however subtle. But what I want to point out most especially can be seen above the sun. Do you, too, see a very realistic eye? Simply look for the darkest part of the upper left quadrant of the photo, which is the pupil of an eye. To the right of it (a bit hard to see) is another much smaller eye, approximately a quarter of the size of the large eye. There have been many occasions I look up and see eyes looking back at me ever since I began my gazing work, where I channel Divine energy through my eyes (www.newsungazing.com). I captured these particular eyes in the sky just one month after I began my new work in August of 2013.

Looking up and documenting the magic in the skies is obviously an important part of what I do, as well. I am seeking—looking up—on a daily basis, literally on a constant basis when outside. Once when hiking on a crisp fall morning, I didn't see anything extraordinary but "heard" a whisper to take a photograph, and this is what was captured. And something here took my breath away.

Do you see the eyebrow, eye, nose, and mouth in the middle of the left side?

The smiley face.

Smiley faces in the sky? Absolutely, I see them all the time.

In this case they are inverted (openings in the clouds) and quite humorous looking. Look for the two animated faces above the two peaks of the mountain. There also appears to be a very happy face seen in the pink array to the right, in the lower part of the picture. The Heavenly realms are always reminding us to smile and feel joy.

The cleanup crew.

Some people might see a "cleanup crew" in here.

Our skies have been changing not only due to the thinning of the veil, but there are many reports and extremely serious concerns of man-made elements being continuously projected into our atmosphere. There is a growing awareness and belief that our skies are generally whiter and often left with lines of chemicals that slowly and eventually diffuse, affecting the earth and everything on it. The subject of chemtrails has been brought up to me by many as a result of sharing my cloud pictures with others. I've been referred to studies and documentaries such as "What in the World Are They Spraying" on YouTube.com. This awareness building among humanity is juxtaposed with reports that we are also getting help and the chemicals are being cleaned up to a degree. Some of us see angelic or galactic representation within the streaks of white, which demonstrates intervention. These beings are showing us they are "cleaning" the skies and ensuring our survival through this period of time. We can choose to assert our free will and request help from the Heavens to help and reverse these actions. My understanding is that our unseen friends "above" can intervene only so much without permission, enough to safeguard our survival, since we are on a planet of free choice. We simply must wake up to the truth.

Life clearly is revealing stunning juxtapositions of both Light and dark, which can leave us feeling, perhaps, confused, while also in awe. I reiterate that we see these polarizing energies not only on earth, but also when we look up, and we decipher the difference. Seeing life continually from a higher, spiritual perspective is what helps us best persevere through these times. We can empower ourselves to stay out of fear—which is immensely key—request Divine intervention with our unwavering trust in God, and continually envision our new, unstoppable, and Heavenly earth that is forming.

A day before sending this book into production, I took a picture of this chemtrail and simply had to include it. I immediately saw a "k" to the far left and felt there was a message. But I got distracted by all the angel beings present, so when I returned home I posted this on a social media site, expressing gratitude for the cleanup. A friend wrote that she saw words and was trying to make them out. This caused me to look closely and I then saw the word "kind." It almost looks like "Kind is ur" and then what appears to be a heart shape. "Kind is your heart"? What do you see?

It just goes to show that we can find beauty, somehow, in most anything. The expression of love and Light, the highest energies of all, always wins. As our beloved earth and all its beings move into higher consciousness, the darkness will eventually be unable to remain.

Here is a striking sunset view. Doesn't it look like there is one being after another, as if in a line dance?

Animals abound.

I'm not sure why I see images of elephants in the sky so often, but I simply do. Are they representing the deity Ganesh, the elephant-headed god? He is known to be the remover of obstacles and since timing often helps to unveil a synchronistic message I consider my present life situation. Or maybe the symbolism is purely connected to qualities of the elephant, reminding one to draw on their inherent strength and wisdom.

Here was one happy looking little fellow.

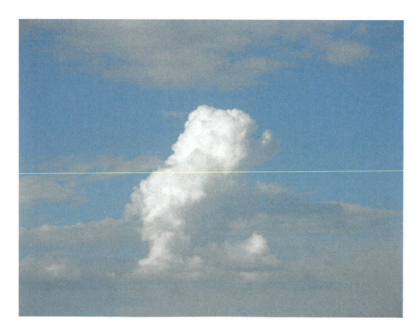

They often look as if in flight—in this case, over Boulder.

There are often clear depictions of dogs' faces up there—well, faces of all kinds of animals, actually—and I feel most definitely that they are often pets who have passed on.

This particular cloud formation appeared in the shape of a dog that looks as if it is fetching a bone or something.

Here is an especially majestic bird that is flaunting quite a wingspan.

Within this depiction are many faces within the shape of his body. Just take your time to seek them out. The more you look, the more you will see.

This bird took flight over Boulder. I often see bird-shaped clouds when looking up. And when I do, I consider… Shall I get ready to "fly?" Do I need to choose freedom from something? Should I see things from a bird's-eye view, meaning from a higher perspective?

Here is a bird-like creature with a very definitive beak that created the sense of movement through the glowing sun.

Birds in general are most definitely powerful messengers from the Heavenly realms. On the morning of my birthday in October of 2014, I went to a favorite hiking trail. There didn't seem to be anything too eventful in the sky. But then a hawk seemed to come out of nowhere, well to the side of me and flew even further away. I telepathically asked it to please come back and fly above me so I could see it better. And it truly did! It turned around and circled directly above me and even made some grand sounds—being close enough for me to see it call. Giving attention to the birds and receiving their messages in endless ways can create such joy.

Hearts.

This heart cloud was seen the same day as my most cherished Jesus cloud, which I shared in Chapter One.

Love in the sky.
Couples appear in the clouds quite often.

Here, they look like they have wings and together form a heart shape. I often see couples represented in the sky, embracing or kissing.

Or, in this case, are these dogs kissing?

Aquatic life.

It's a thrill to see dolphin and whale-shaped clouds "swimming" in the sky. When you look closely, you appreciate the detail. Here you may see a dolphin's nose, head, body, fins, and tail.

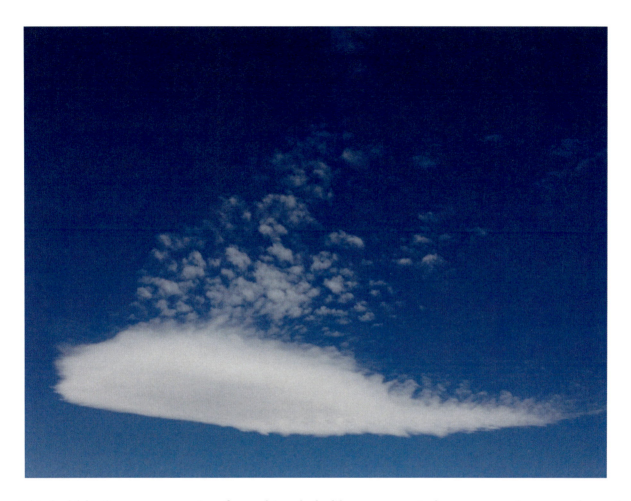

"Air bubbles" are seen coming from this whale-like creature. I always appreciate any photo that depicts a darker blue sky; something we aren't seeing very often. But in reality, it probably wasn't this blue. Sometimes when I tap my iPhone camera display in order to focus on any one thing, and especially when photographing around the sun, it often presents a darker background than what I actually see; there doesn't seem to be a way around that.

When I saw this spectacle, I wanted to belt out: "When that shark bites, with his teeth, dear," from the song "Mack the Knife."

This beauty displayed extraordinary movement and perfection. It looks as if it's performing a back dive into the water.

Luck and manifestation.

Who doesn't love a symbol of good luck, whether it's a four-leaf clover, a ladybug, or even a magic lamp?

Of the many times I've spotted clouds looking like magic lamps, this is probably my favorite. It seemed almost close enough to touch.

Famous faces.

I love when I look up and sense recognition of the faces I see.

When I saw that Einstein cloud (in Chapter One), my heart opened up to a whole new world of possibilities of what we see when we look up. Can the spirits of famous people who have passed actually reveal their likeness in clouds? I saw Charlie Chaplin's face in the sun the moment I downloaded this picture above. Could it really be him, or was I fetching? When I shared this photo with my friend Lisa, and without saying a word, she immediately said it looked like Charlie Chaplin!

Something astonishing also happened in the sky with regards to the soul known to many as the "King of Pop." Let me first backtrack to the day that Michael Jackson died. I was out driving during the time he passed, that afternoon. I heard the words "heart attack" clearly in my mind, and it took my breath away for a moment. Was there something wrong with me and was I being warned? I seemed fine. So why did I hear those words? When I returned home, I immediately understood what that message was about. I was shocked by the growing news reports I read online that Michael Jackson had suffered cardiac arrest, and then died.

Two days later, my friend Maria Weber, from Colorado, emailed me a photograph that her husband Jim captured of the sunset on June 27, 2009. After he took it, Maria looked in the camera display and immediately saw the image of Michael Jackson in those clouds. It took me a moment to see what she saw too, and since then, I see him so clearly. I had no question that this was Michael saying "Hello" to the world, and letting us know that he was fine at a time when millions deeply mourned his sudden passing.

Photo by Jim Bassett

Look for one of the darker parts of the photo—just above and slightly left of the very center—and you will see his hair. From there you will see him lengthwise, as if floating, with his body to the right of his head.

It was no coincidence that my friends not only showed me this picture, but also generously gave me permission to share their photo since. I was feeling quite an intense connection to Michael since the day he passed, even though I was never a big fan of his. I had great respect for his talent and knew most of his songs, but I didn't even own one of his CDs—unlike most fans of Michael.

However, in the months following his transition I heard his music in my head so often, sometimes several times throughout the day. For instance, I would wake with the words from Michael's "Human Nature" on my lips, and still hear it hours later. Whenever we randomly hear songs in our heads, there is surely reason behind it. Our higher selves or beings from Heaven may be whispering a tune (telepathically, with or without our knowing) for a clue or message. So it is helpful to consider the lyrics to decipher the meaning relative to you.

After I posted an article on hubpages.com about these experiences regarding Michael, including this special photograph, several people shared similar experiences with me. The number of comments and even personal emails I received from people also having similar intense feelings of connection with the spirit of Michael Jackson, as well, amazed me. While I felt a sudden deep desire to learn more about him, to understand what was really going on in his life—beyond the rumors, scandals, and sensationalism—I quickly learned that I wasn't alone in this quest.

When I saw the televised interview of Deepak Chopra, who was close friends with Michael, discussing Michael and their friendship, it opened a window to that understanding. I feel there are so many messages that he conveyed through his music, and accentuated since his passing, about love vs. hate, about suffering, about judgment and how we treat each other, and about truth and how things aren't always what they seem. His messages seemed to ultimately be about love, or the unveiling of love as our only truth. I believe that Michael is continuing his mission from another dimension to help humanity, along with scores of other souls.

Things are simply not as they seem, certainly when we consider and ponder the truths of our metaphysical existence on this planet. And surely when it comes to looking up at our sky. Most of us human beings, too busy being humans, would look up right now and see nothing different. Yet we have the choice to open our hearts and see—really see—from that place, and glean from the messages of the clouds. We need to lessen the hold on those belief systems so heavily entrenched in us—thinking we know more than we really do, or erroneously believing that things will always be the same, including up there in the sky. Because nothing could be further from the truth in our rapidly evolving world. When we have the courage to reassess our beliefs and possibly reassign new ones, we go with the flow of beneficial change, rather than against it.

CHAPTER FIVE:
SOME EXTRAORDINARY PUFFS OF WHITE

May these clouds inspire you to further seek unending awe when you look up.

The extraordinary visuals can take our breath away. They take us out of the daily grind and make us stop, view, and feel, as we listen to the language of the skies. We look up and see something so much bigger than ourselves that it can leave us in awe. This particular one that seemed to be filled with an intense amount of energy amazed some viewers and frightened others.

Some believe that certain cloud formations are actually cloaking spaceships. Next, you'll see a few images to ponder in this way, perhaps. I saw the following wonder in Nederland, Colorado.

This spectacular sunset display was captured right from my front porch. I wasn't the only one who thought that something was hiding in there. When online the next day, I "happened" to come across a similar picture of this cloud taken from a Denver vantage point, and the accompanying article questioned if there was some kind of spaceship hiding in there.

Something significant seems to be going on behind all of this white, distinguished by a lovely, small rainbow.

What made this especially striking was that this cloud in Boulder on December 6, 2014 was hovering right over a protest of several hundred people decrying racism. I was unaware of the protest when I saw this cloud from my window at home. I was guided to "Leave now!" and continued to view it for the ten-minute drive into town. Once there, I found myself literally in the middle of this protest that stopped traffic on both sides of the road. I immediately felt that everyone was being observed and watched over.

Sometimes the sun looks like a big eye, especially when fused with the clouds just so.

This is one of my more unique captures. While it may be considered somewhat ominous, this array of clouds appears to create an image of a butterfly which isn't ominous at all.

Love shows itself in endless ways, sometimes through a beautiful montage of sky with land.

The closer you look, the more extraordinary you may deem this one.

Do you see a profile of a woman? Eyes, nose, neck, hair, and even teeth? And, yet, there are also scores of faces within her "portrait."

You'd think a convention was taking place up there, with all of these faces grouped together. In fact, both this and the previous photo offer great opportunities to practice finding the faces. Once again, really take your time and just allow the faces come into view.

Sometimes I look up and find out I am actually receiving a sign for someone else, such as when I saw this cloud.

My friend Elina St Clair and I have the same guide from the Heavenly realms. It was Elina who introduced me to him. On a summer day in 2013, she had just received a sign from him when at the swimming pool with her children (a thousand miles away from me) at the very same time I spotted this cloud, as it turned out. We were talking on the phone shortly after when she told me of her sign, and I then shared this photo. Do you get the sense that this being is swimming too? Elina sure did. And, in fact, it proved to be very meaningful to her.

And this same friend, soon after receiving a channeled message about a past king, logged onto a social media site. She saw my photo below and knew exactly who this was. It served as another confirming message for Elina. And, interestingly, I thought of her the moment I saw this cloud.

Do you see a crowned and bearded king holding a baby with a halo? I am convinced that we can receive messages of validation for each other via the skies, as well as in a multitude of ways.

CHAPTER SIX:
THE NEW SUN IS CHANGING THE SKIES

What is causing the skies to change? I am not a scientist, but I do have very strong feelings and unique understandings about this subject. Well, to be specific, I have an angel on my shoulder who is giving me a heads up about what's going on up there. As mentioned, I am a channel of Archangel Michael. Ever since 2001, our beautiful archangel has provided me with messages all about where we are headed—our creation of a Heavenly earth where we move into a higher consciousness and a new way of being. Yes, a whole new paradigm of living. We can see with our own eyes that this is real by simply looking up. We see that the veils have thinned and Heaven and earth are merging.

While some of us completely believe that the world is changing for the better, others either don't or are unaware of the bigger picture. There is so much chaos in the world now and this strongly challenges us to consider that we are actually headed in a most positive direction despite the way things look. We will rise from the chaos. The world will run on the energy of love—we will live from our hearts, and, thus, know what peace feels like.

In order for this to happen, there is a Sun behind the sun that we know, what Michael refers to as the "New Sun." He describes it this way in my book *The New Sun* [2]:

> This New Sun is also referred to as the Great Central Sun, and although it is not a new sun to us—as it is the sun that is our source in the Heavenly realms—it is new to you.

Michael goes on to explain:

> The New Sun is shining and exuding the new Light, and this is changing everything on your earth. Every single thing will be affected by the new Light. It is already happening.

---

[2] Soliel, Mary. *The New Sun: With Archangel Michael*. Boulder: Twelve Twelve Publishing, LLC, 2013.

So, is Michael referring to the skies too? Absolutely. By looking up, we see the signs of these changes. As the veils thin between Heaven and earth, and as the new Light builds and raises the vibration of this planet, we are literally seeing the changes in the sky. And specifically in the clouds, as you have witnessed throughout this book.

The New Sun is transforming the effects and presence of the sun that you have known as third dimensional beings. It's as if there is this new metaphysical template in the sky, and with the veil thinning, we are utilizing a closer connection with you now, via your very skies. The New Sun makes this possible. Think of it this way: with the creation of this new template, it allows us to work in a synergistic way with you and connect with you, such as through the magical clouds you are now seeing, with faces "painted" on them.

Michael said to me:

Mary, you do think of us as painting your skies, and that is certainly a way to look at it. We are expressing ourselves through the sky as if it were a canvas.

I was very intrigued to hear what Archangel Michael had to say about new colors appearing in our atmosphere:

Are you noticing the new colors yet? There are actually new colors that are being beamed to you and there is reason behind this. Color carries energy, and as you continue to raise your vibrations, you are able to see colors that could not be perceived by your eyes before. When you begin to see new colors they are another signal to you that you are shifting. Do not worry if you do not see them; you eventually will.

Many of us are seeing rainbow colors framing, or within, the clouds—particularly clouds that are situated close to the sun. Because it is often too bright to see, one may appreciate them best by snapping a picture of the colorful displays.

The colors can make an ordinary cloud look quite mesmerizing. This cloud also seems to reveal an eye, even eyes within an eye if you look closely. The eye as a symbol is connected to the Divine, and that is how I always choose to attract it—even though the single eye is used in far less than holy symbolism, as well. Many holy names and symbols are used by the extreme opposite of holy, sadly, but we can easily discern the difference. When I see an eye as a Divine symbol, it means so many things to me; most especially that we are being supremely watched over. I also think of what is known to be our all-seeing third eye and the pineal gland. This cloud is one that you can ponder for some time and see new things.

It's quite magical when the sun can be captured with a rainbow around it.

As mentioned, these large magenta orbs that you've seen in this book, and often included with a tiny whitish green or blue orb within it, appear in many people's solar captures taken with the iPhone. It makes for a very colorful picture.

Sometimes I achieve a special effect when photographing the sun through tree branches, allowing just the right amount of light in to create a beautiful composition. Taken near Cathedral Rock in Sedona, Arizona, this photo reveals a rainbow around the sun along with brilliant colored orbs from turquoise to royal blue.

Inverted clouds can be most interesting and revealing.

To me, this is clearly an arrow pointing at the star of the show… the Sun! Many of us are naturally gravitating our attention toward our solar star, and it is partly because the skies are guiding that gravitation in a variety of ways. We are also intuiting that our sun is exhibiting something new.

Sun halos are always eye-catching. They are known to be composed of ice crystals that form a ring around the sun. Rainbow colors that make up the halo may or may not be visible. This circular phenomenon can also be seen around the moon—known as lunar halos.

However, these sun halos are also known to be called "chembows," as well, which claims that they are caused by chemtrails. Again, I'm neither a scientist or a meteorologist, so I'm not sure in every case what are normal expressions in the atmosphere, or what is Heaven versus human influenced (or a mixture, thereof). I am an observer who is reporting the changes above. Even prior to the millennium, I recall increased sightings of rainbow spots and intuitively felt they were a sign that the skies were changing.

Specifically, I cannot ascertain what colors, or clouds for that matter, are results of the shifting energies versus what are results of human influence from geoengineering. If it is the latter, I see the conflicting dichotomy similar to the theory that air pollution can actually enhance a sunset. Is ugliness transmuted into a beautiful array to witness? These times can be confusing, no doubt.

You simply need to "Ask and ye shall receive." I asked the angels for another heart-shaped cloud, and on the same day saw not only a heart shaped glow from the sun, but along with remarkable coloring. And some special faces too.

Minutes later it looked like this.

I'm often driven to capture clouds against the sun (from our perspective) since I regularly achieve magical, even angelic results.

At a time when dolphins seemed to be in my awareness from so many sources, I saw this rainbow dolphin head in the sky.

This photo taken of the sun's rays by my friend and gifted photographer Elina is utterly breathtaking. Clearly, the sun and the skies are revealing unprecedented displays of wonder and magnificence.

Photo by Elina St Clair

When capturing the sun's gifts as seen through the vantage point of beautiful Naples, Florida, I came across this stunning wash of violet light.

I was extremely surprised by what I captured through the trees during this particular sunrise. The camera picked up a much more enticing image than my own eyes did. Of course, considering it's the bright sun which we shouldn't be looking directly at, maybe that is to be expected.

Getting the sun in on the capture can prove magical, as seen by the following examples. I like to call these "solar selfies."

We have entered the "selfie" age, as social media promotes. When I filmed some videos of my channeled messages (as seen on YouTube.com, on the "MarySoliel" channel) when in Sedona in 2012, I was amazed to see an abundance of rays in front of my face (with the sun behind me). So I then learned to angle my phone camera towards me with the sun as the backdrop, and capture the presentation of orbs, rays, and colors. It led to another way of exploring the changing energies from the sun. Now I often take solar selfies to see what colors, rays, and orbs show up from time to time.

As mentioned, I'm known to regularly pull over and stop the car, to capture something I find alluring and magical in the sky. Clouds can change so quickly. This image serves as a great example as I initially saw what looked like an angel bowing to the sun. But, by the time I stopped the car, the image transformed completely.

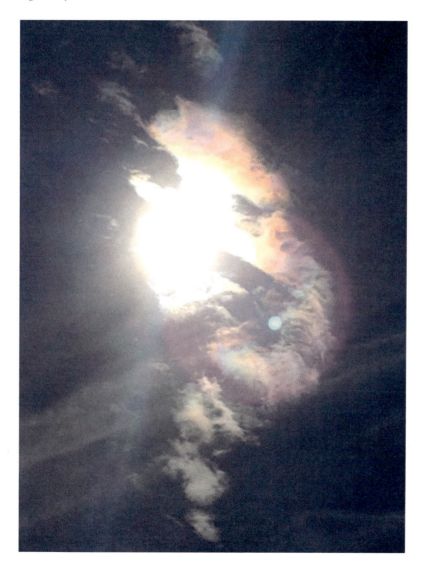

Even the rainbows themselves seem different, don't they? It appears that there are more full and double rainbows and are seen for longer periods of time. I witnessed this full double rainbow for ninety minutes (the full rainbow didn't surface that whole time, but at least parts of it). And I saw a repetition of the spectrum of colors, doubling or even tripling the sequence at times. I sense there may be new colors there, but I cannot see them yet.

CHAPTER SEVEN:
LOOK UP, LOOK DOWN, LOOK ALL AROUND

What we see when we look up is also seen in different ways when we look down, sideways, or any which way. It's just that instead of a message or face in the form of water and ice suspended in air—what we call a cloud—we see a vast variety of symbolism through things such as a personalized license plate, meaningful numbers on a clock, and all kinds of surprises from nature. And these gems can synchronistically provide messages in endless ways. Heaven truly can and does reveal itself through anything. So while this book is about looking up, as a new phenomenon has unveiled itself in the skies, I highly recommend you look everywhere else for the blessings, too. They are often connected by validating and emphasizing similar messages.

For instance, imagine looking up and catching sight of a lovely rainbow. Then you look down and find a few coins right in front of your feet. After picking them up, you see just ahead a money truck driving toward you. All these events may be a glorious combination of signs signaling a turning point in your financial abundance and prompting you to stop doing what too many of us do—worry about money. Expect astronomical odds in messengers such as these coming together to mirror your beautiful life, and the potentials of your future. On top of that, our angels, and even passed loved ones, not only use synchronicity to communicate to us, but they can also manipulate all kinds of matter. One common way they do this is to leave coins on your path, by the way. I discuss this subject in my other books.

It takes a watchful eye and a playful heart to see and appreciate the signs. You must allow yourself to see things simply and at face value. Be a clear and open observer of how life presents itself to you. Just as with the clouds, always consider the timing of the wonder compared to what is going on in your life, and especially what is in your powerful thoughts in that exact moment.

Not only do I see exclamation point-shaped clouds when I look up, but check out what I saw so perfectly positioned when looking down during a leisurely hike.

Here's a little sign a birdie seemed to deposit so perfectly on a rock. The source of the message can sometimes make one laugh.

When walking around a lake in Louisville, Colorado, after a rain, a puddle shaped as the powerful number 8 (infinity sign, also) was perfectly illuminated by the sun.

My daughter, Karen, came across this random "work of art" on a sidewalk which proved to be very meaningful. Being a brilliant healer and artist, she is in very close connection with the angelic realms.

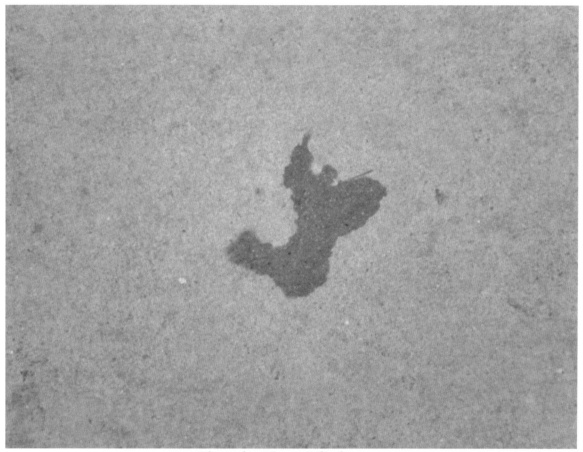

Photo by Karen Kliethermes

Do you, too, see that the water mark is in the shape of an angel? It was quite a lively, detailed, and even musical pose created out of a splash of water on the ground!

The Universe—often through nature, yet, in many endless ways—reminds us again and again to just be love. Seeing this simple and beautifully intricate arrangement truly reset my day. Beauty can be easily dismissed, but we can train ourselves to observe as much as possible and make the connections, to our immense benefit. You probably know just what I speak of.

Signs can even arrive through unique shapes of fruits and vegetables. This must have mirrored my mood on one particular day! At least her third eye is opening (…laughing).

When I pulled out of a plastic bag a couple of lemon cucumbers I bought at the Boulder Farmer's Market, my daughter noticed the shape I left the opening of that bag in… of a heart. Immediately after that, she looked at the peaches soaking in the sink tub and saw a live ladybug on one of the peaches. Coincidence? Not in our view. The fact that hearts and ladybugs are among our favorite positive signs made for an especially enjoyable few moments.

A random dollop of hummus on a carrot created something most intricate and unique.

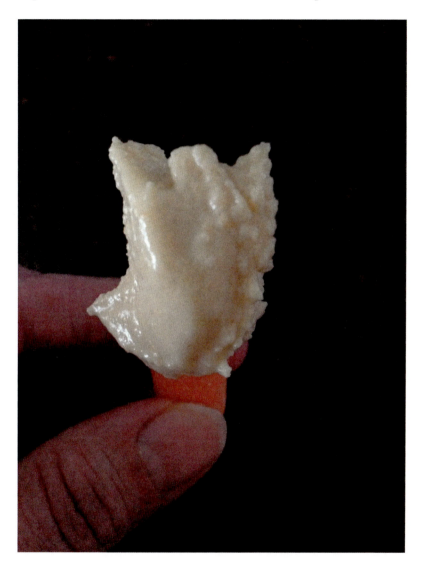

Do you see a winged angel, too?

Hearts can be seen most everywhere; in clouds, foods, and even rock shapes.

When I came across this rock on October 1, 2014, I posted this picture on social media with the message: "Just in... Forecast for October: Perpetual smiles, sunshine, and lots of love!"

"Well, hello there!" Thanks for the wave.

    The bell-shaped rock on the next page made quite an impression on me when I spotted it while hiking on September 26, 2014 in Boulder. As soon as I saw the rock, I was reminded of a little miracle that Archangel Michael delivered during my speaking event in New Mexico in November of 2013. Let me share with you what happened on that magical day.

I was taking a little drive to clear my mind before my full day of speaking when Michael came through with a brief message. He simply said, "Listen for the bells." When Diane Camillo, the owner of Awaken to Wellness Center in Albuquerque, brought up tingsha bells during my talk, I immediately shared with everyone what Michael had said that morning. Then just minutes later, a bell rang all on its own in the room! It was hanging above the door, but at that time no one walked in and there was no rush of air causing the bell to move. We all looked towards the door and laughed, realizing it was Michael. His timing was impeccable—not only after I brought up his words to me, but also right after I described ways in which our angels influence matter.

Sometimes signs can have us relive previous miracles and memories for some unknown reason, or, perhaps, for many reasons. In fact, this wondrous synchronicity actually prompted me to spontaneously schedule another speaking event in Albuquerque. Do I feel that this was Archangel Michael's perfect and magical way to send me a sign that it was time for a return visit? Indeed. It proved to be yet another memorable event.

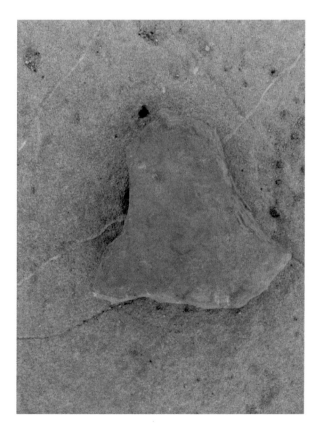

On August 30, 2014, my daughter and I went to the Denver Botanical Gardens. We had just sat down to have lunch at the outdoor bistro and something flew right in my face and then landed on my napkin... a little blue dragonfly. I sensed I should put my finger out toward it, somehow knowing that it would climb up my finger. And it indeed climbed up and remained there for a while.

Photo by Karen Kliethermes

The dragonfly then flew onto my arm and with its blue eyes looked right into my eyes for several minutes. People around us couldn't get over the way it was looking directly at me, including us. It stayed with me for at least ten minutes. Never before had I experienced anything like this. I know that "someone from above" was behind this, knowing that I would share with you here. Of course, things happen for so many reasons, but this was definitely one of them.

Photo by Karen Kliethermes

As you may know, the dragonfly is a symbol for transformation, which is what we are all experiencing quite intensely now. Nature sure is a most magical validator through animals, insects, trees, water, rocks, clouds, rainbows, the sun—all of it.

Even inanimate, man-made objects can serve as extraordinary signs. Since moving to Colorado, I often meet up with the Pioneer trucks at the most perfect moments. The synchronicities mirror the need to embrace my role, our roles, as pioneers discovering our quietly unfolding new world.

This message was reinforced on a winter day when I saw this truck. After driving by it, I "heard" to go around the block again. When I did, I saw that a second Pioneer truck was just getting behind the first and then they both followed behind me. It was extra reinforcement to behold and celebrate. It's time to embrace the wonderment and gift of being pioneers now, right now, as we are in these times. What messages are you attracting on this very day?

The symbolism of a mere balloon can brighten one's day a thousandfold, given circumstances such as this. I was walking down the hallway toward my kids' rooms starting to explain how I just saw the most amazing shooting star outside. And before I had the chance to say "shooting star," my magical son walks out of his room with this in his hands. It was a balloon I gave him several months prior, that was sitting in his closet! He unknowingly magnified an already wonderful sign.

These are a sampling of the remarkable, endless ways the Universe mirrors messages for us, and often in combination with looking up. Being tuned in to the possibilities makes life much more thrilling and mystical, and helps us ease through these challenging times in our world.

CHAPTER EIGHT:
THE ULTIMATE GIFT IN LOOKING UP

The instantaneous joy and wonderment that arise from looking up have been demonstrated throughout this book. But the ultimate gift, in my opinion, is quiet and unfolding. I believe that the skies are moving us further toward our spiritual evolution. As I stated earlier, by merely acknowledging the magic and miracles in the sky, we raise our energetic vibrations. We are also releasing the third dimensional aspects of ourselves, as we grow closer to our souls—who we *really* are. This is why many of us are facing such drama, having beliefs and behaviors that no longer serve us "in our faces" now so that we learn, forgive, and truly let go. Everyone and everything is being "elevated," so to speak, as we create our Heavenly earth.

Let's face it. There are too many unspeakable, chaotic, and disheartening atrocities occurring on our beautiful planet, and it's not always easy being here and witnessing the negative acts and their repercussions. Again, part of our spiritual awakening is being aware of not only spiritual truths, but also the reality of the difficult to absorb low vibrational truths of greed, corruption, and power in the hands of those who have harmed our earth and all who reside on it. We obtain this awareness so that we can transcend this reality with understanding and relentless faith. We can choose to stay positive and trust that we are moving toward a Heavenly earth as the darkness continues to fall. We can be aware, make good choices, take action to reassess, renew, and rebuild—all while maintaining that higher perspective so that we stay away from fear… the opposite of love.

Love is what is saving the planet. We are individually and collectively moving further into love and learning to just be love. As we move out of our ego driven minds and more into our hearts to embrace heart-centered living, we truly change the world into a peaceful and abundant one. We are already doing this. How can one tell? Just look up. Heaven is reflecting the love that we are.

No one says it better than Archangel Michael, in *Michael's Clarion Call* [3]:

Yes, think of it in this way: your sky is reflecting the rising beauty coming from earth's inhabitants. As things change below, they change above, as well. Again, I say look up, perceive, and enjoy what the skies are telling you.

[3] Soliel, Mary. *Michael's Clarion Call: Messages from the Archangel for Creating Heaven on Earth.* Boulder: Twelve Twelve Publishing, LLC, 2011.

On October 2, 1994, a Divine white light came into my right eye, marked the beginning of my spiritual journey, and changed me forevermore. On the evening of my 17th anniversary of this event, I was guided to visit Marshall Lake in Louisville, Colorado, where I snapped this picture. I had walked around this lake countless times prior, but never captured it like this. It was surreal. Michael wanted me to match this remarkable display of nature with his words preceding the photo. He explained that they went well together. So may we embrace our movement into love and relish in the reflection of the skies. Heaven is reflecting the love that we are. Look around. It is everywhere.

Michael also told me several years ago that animals in the wild will not be so wild. *Watch how life in the wild will also evolve to mirror the new ways of the human. (Michael's Clarion Call)* Are we not seeing this now? Humanity is demonstrating rising love and compassion toward animals, and animals are exhibiting more love and compassion toward each other (including inter-species), as well as toward humans. We are all mirrors for each other and all things, and love is the driving force that brings us all together.

I synchronistically came across some beautiful words from Miguel Ruiz that mirror what Michael has shared with me. In *The Four Agreements* [4] he says: "What you will see is love coming out of the trees, love coming out of the sky, love coming out of the light. You will perceive love from everything around you. This is the state of bliss."

This is something I believe to be so beautiful and true. Love is where it's at. All this talk about love is not fluffy or invented; it is real. It has Heaven's stamp on it. This is a promise of unprecedented change when we choose love. So next time you look up, know that you are actively participating in our evolution into love in a most conscious manner.

---

[4] Ruiz, Don Miguel. *The Four Agreements: A Practical Guide to Personal Freedom.* San Rafael: Amber-Allen Publishing, 1997.

ABOUT THE AUTHOR

Mary Soliel is an author, visionary, speaker, gazer, and self-described "synchronist." Her three-time award-winning book, *I Can See Clearly Now: How Synchronicity Illuminates Our Lives,* is a groundbreaking exploration of the phenomenon of synchronicity.

As a channel of Archangel Michael, the publishing of *Michael's Clarion Call: Messages from the Archangel for Creating Heaven on Earth* and *The New Sun: With Archangel Michael* highlight Mary's mission as a teacher and messenger to globally raise awareness of the Golden Age before us. Both titles are also award-winning, and considered to be life changing reads, as well.

Mary's fourth book *Look Up!* demonstrates her pioneering exploration and visual proof of our movement toward a new and Heavenly earth. Mary is available for U.S. and international speaking engagements and radio/print/television interviews. Please visit her at: **www.marysoliel.com** and **www.newsungazing.com**.

Made in the USA
Monee, IL
15 November 2024

70226303R00081